SQUARE
A PIZZA BOX OR A CHECKERBOARD

By SYDNEY LEPEW

Illustrated by ANNIE WILKENSON

CANTATA
LEARNING
MANKATO, MINNESOTA

WWW.CANTATALEARNING.COM

CANTATA LEARNING

MANKATO, MINNESOTA

Published by Cantata Learning
1710 Roe Crest Drive
North Mankato, MN 56003
www.cantatalearning.com

Library of Congress Control Number: 2014957007
978-1-63290-274-0 (hardcover/CD)
978-1-63290-426-3 (paperback/CD)
978-1-63290-468-3 (paperback)

Square: A Pizza Box or a Checkerboard by Sydney LePew
Illustrated by Annie Wilkinson

Book design, Tim Palin Creative
Editorial direction, Flat Sole Studio
Executive musical production and direction, Elizabeth Draper
Music produced by Wes Schuck
Audio recorded, mixed, and mastered at Two Fish Studios, Mankato, MN

Printed in the United States of America.

VISIT
WWW.CANTATALEARNING.COM/ACCESS-OUR-MUSIC
TO SING ALONG TO THE SONG

A square is a shape with four sides.

A square is made up of four lines.

Each line is the same length.

Where two of the lines meet,

there is a **right angle**.

Now turn the page,

and sing along.

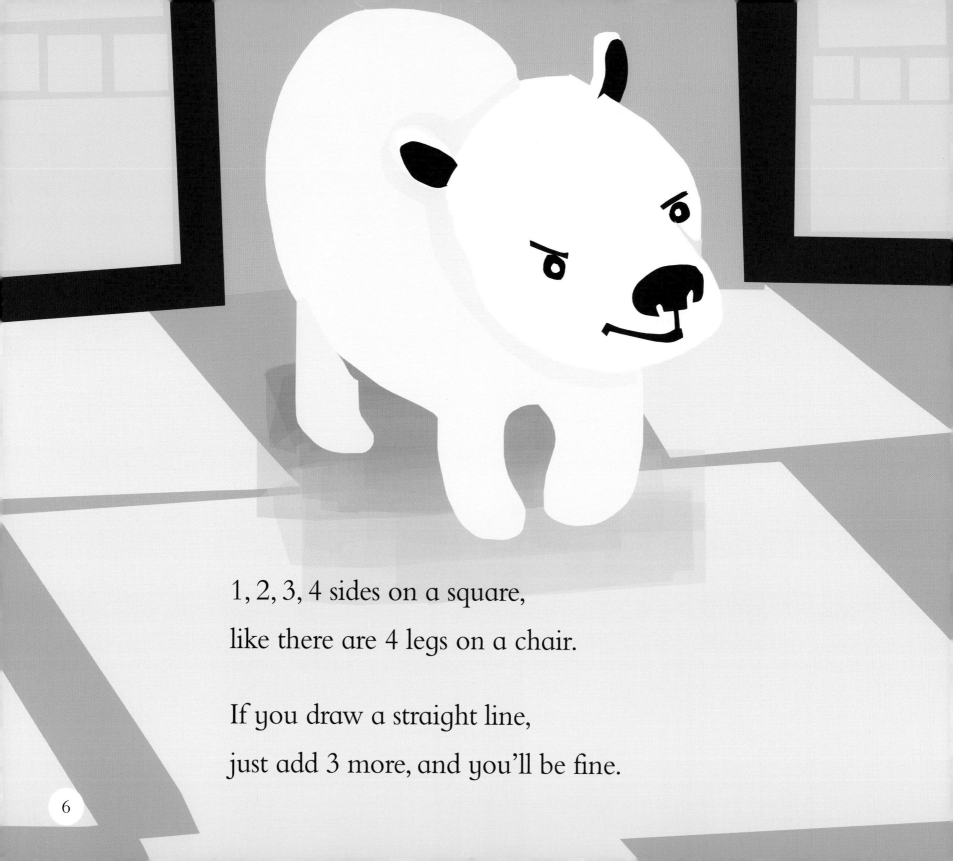

1, 2, 3, 4 sides on a square,

like there are 4 legs on a chair.

If you draw a straight line,

just add 3 more, and you'll be fine.

It's easier than wrestling a bear!

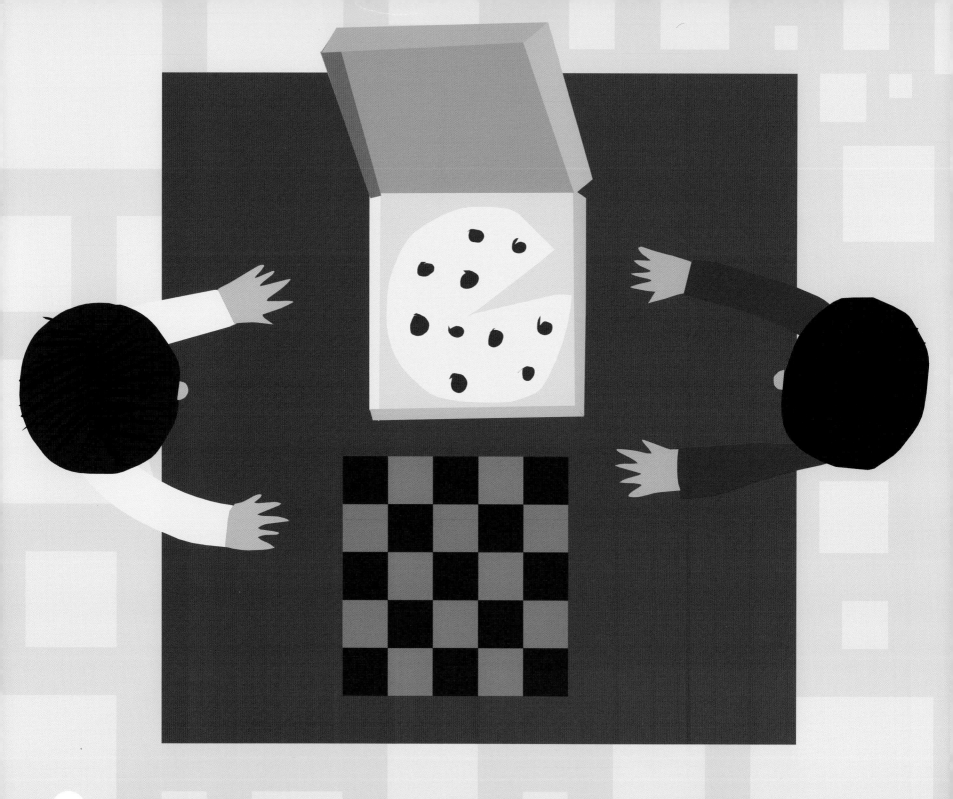

If you look, you'll see them everywhere.
The top of a pizza box is square.

Square tiles across the bathroom floor,
and colored squares on a checkerboard.

9

Playing hopscotch on the ground,
squares are where the fun is found.

If you're hungry, just look around.
Crackers are tasty squares to gobble down.

CRACKER CRACKER
SQUARES SQUARES

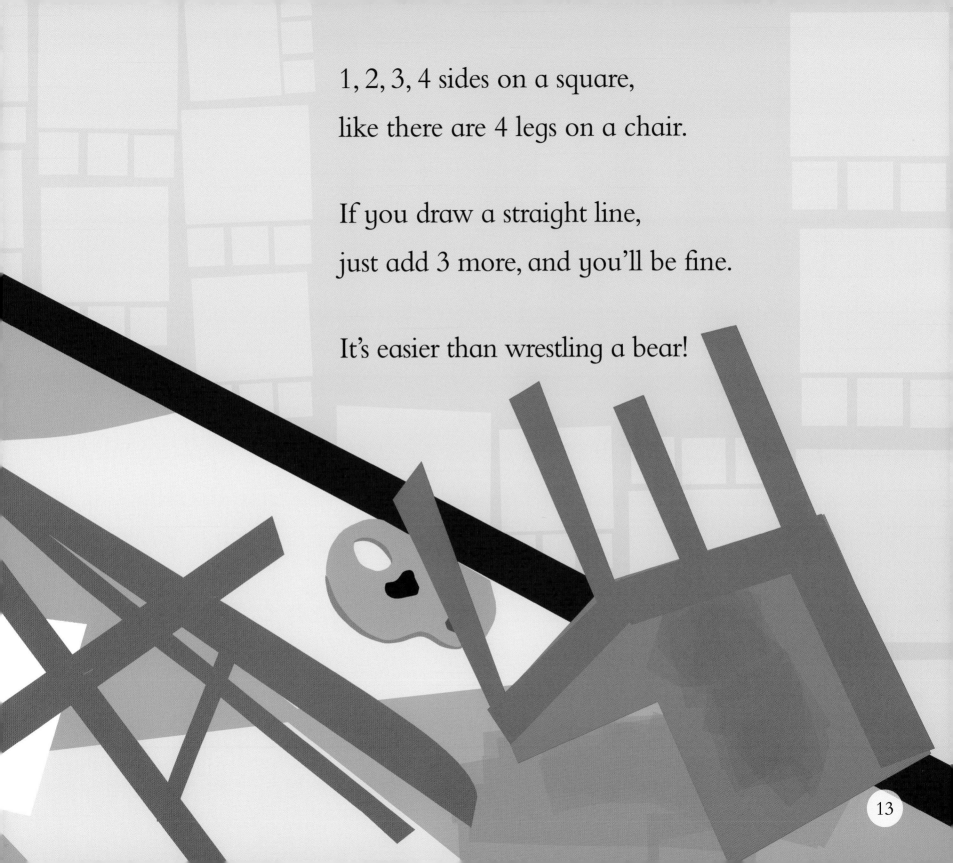

1, 2, 3, 4 sides on a square,

like there are 4 legs on a chair.

If you draw a straight line,

just add 3 more, and you'll be fine.

It's easier than wrestling a bear!

There's a picture on the wall.

The frame is square, and that's not all.

A big square window to see outside.

Wooden blocks are piled up to the sky.

A square is a kind of rectangle,
but not all rectangles are a square.
Look at them and compare.

They both have four sides.
A rectangle's can be long and short
while a square's are all one size.

18

When I'm dreaming in my bed,
a lot of shapes float around my head.

Circles, stars, and triangles are there,
but none is shaped quite like a square.

1, 2, 3, 4 sides on a square,

like there are 4 legs on a chair.

If you draw a straight line,

just add 3 more, and you'll be fine.

It's easier than wrestling a bear!

SONG LYRICS
Square: A Pizza Box or a Checkerboard

1, 2, 3, 4 sides on a square,
like there are 4 legs on a chair.

If you draw a straight line,
just add 3 more, and you'll be fine.

It's easier than wrestling a bear!

If you look, you'll see them everywhere.
The top of a pizza box is square.

Square tiles across the bathroom floor,
and colored squares on a checkerboard.

Playing hopscotch on the ground,
squares are where the fun is found.

If you're hungry, just look around.
Crackers are tasty squares to gobble down.

1, 2, 3, 4 sides on a square,
like there are 4 legs on a chair.

If you draw a straight line,
just add 3 more, and you'll be fine.

It's easier than wrestling a bear!

There's a picture on the wall.
The frame is square, and that's not all.

A big square window to see outside.
Wooden blocks are piled up to the sky.

A square is a kind of rectangle,
but not all rectangles are a square.
Look at them and compare.

They both have four sides.
A rectangle's can be long and short
while a square's are all one size.

When I'm dreaming in my bed,
a lot of shapes float around my head.

Circles, stars, and triangles are there,
but none is shaped quite like a square.

1, 2, 3, 4 sides on a square,
like there are 4 legs on a chair.

If you draw a straight line,
just add 3 more, and you'll be fine.

It's easier than wrestling a bear!

Pop
Wes Schuck

Square: A Pizza Box or a Checkerboard

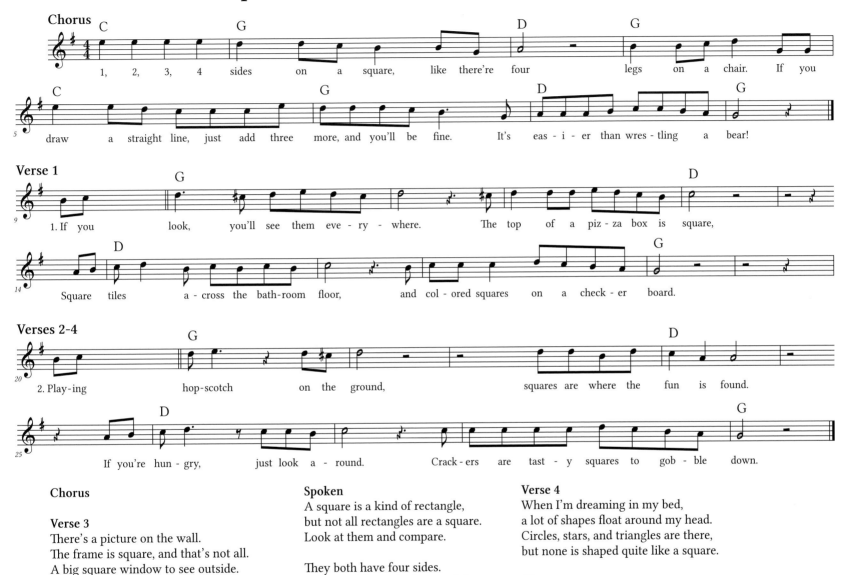

Chorus

1, 2, 3, 4 sides on a square, like there're four legs on a chair. If you draw a straight line, just add three more, and you'll be fine. It's eas-i-er than wres-tling a bear!

Verse 1

1. If you look, you'll see them eve-ry-where. The top of a piz-za box is square, Square tiles a-cross the bath-room floor, and col-ored squares on a check-er board.

Verses 2-4

2. Play-ing hop-scotch on the ground, squares are where the fun is found. If you're hun-gry, just look a-round. Crack-ers are tast-y squares to gob-ble down.

Chorus

Verse 3
There's a picture on the wall.
The frame is square, and that's not all.
A big square window to see outside.
Wooden blocks are piled up to the sky.

Spoken
A square is a kind of rectangle,
but not all rectangles are a square.
Look at them and compare.

They both have four sides.
A rectangle's can be long and short
while a square's are all one size.

Verse 4
When I'm dreaming in my bed,
a lot of shapes float around my head.
Circles, stars, and triangles are there,
but none is shaped quite like a square.

Chorus

GLOSSARY

angle—the space where two lines meet

right angle—the corner of a square

GUIDED READING ACTIVITIES

1. Draw a square. How many lines did you use to make a square?

2. What are some things around you that are shaped like a square?

3. Name three things from this book that are shaped like a square. How do you know they are squares?

TO LEARN MORE

Dilkes, D.H. *I See Squares*. Berkeley Heights, NJ: Enslow Pub. 2011.

Ghigna, Charles. *Shapes Are Everywhere!* North Mankato, MN: Picture Window Books, 2014.

Loughrey, Anita. *Squares*. Irvine, CA: QEB Pub., 2010.

Smith, Mary-Lou. *I See Squares*. New York: Cavendish Square Publishing, 2015.